THE AFRICAN ELEPHANT

BY COLLEEN SEXTON

BELLWETHER MEDIA • MINNEAPOLIS, MN

Jump into the cockpit and take flight with Pilot Books. Your journey will take you on high-energy adventures as you learn about all that is wild, weird, fascinating, and fun!

This edition first published in 2012 by Bellwether Media, Inc.

No part of this publication may be reproduced in whole or in part without written permission of the publisher. For information regarding permission, write to Bellwether Media, Inc., Attention: Permissions Department, 5357 Penn Avenue South, Minneapolis, MN 55419.

Library of Congress Cataloging-in-Publication Data

Sexton, Colleen A., 1967-
 The African elephant / by Colleen Sexton.
  p. cm. – (Pilot books. Nature's deadliest)
 Includes bibliographical references and index.
 Summary: "Fascinating images accompany information about the African elephant. The combination of high-interest subject matter and narrative text is intended for students in grades 3 through 7"–Provided by publisher.
 ISBN 978-1-60014-662-6 (hardcover : alk. paper)
 1. African elephant–Juvenile literature. I. Title.
 QL737.P98S488 2012
 599.67'4-dc22   2011012515

Printed in the United States of America, North Mankato, MN.

080111   1187

CONTENTS

Trampled and Gored

A small group of people was traveling through Kenya in eastern Africa. While setting up camp one day, the group saw an African elephant disappear into some nearby bushes. The campers decided to follow the elephant and spy on it from a safe distance. When they reached the place where they had seen the elephant, they heard a noise. The elephant burst out of the bushes, **trumpeting** loudly. The enormous animal was headed straight toward them!

Charge!

Elephants can run up to 25 miles (40 kilometers) per hour when they are frightened or angry.

The campers ran in different directions. The elephant followed 24-year-old Jonathan Sykes, charging after him at full speed. Behind him, Jonathan could hear the elephant's giant feet pounding the ground. He zigzagged through an area of thorn bushes, hoping the tight turns would slow the elephant down. Despite its size, the elephant was fast. It quickly caught up to Jonathan.

The elephant knocked Jonathan down with its heavy trunk. Jonathan stayed on the ground and curled his body into a ball. The elephant batted him with its **tusks**. It kicked Jonathan several times, moving him a total of about 50 feet (15 meters). Then the elephant thrust a tusk at him. The tusk tore Jonathan's calf muscle in half.

The smell of Jonathan's blood was in the air. The elephant poked him with its foot. Jonathan kept very still and pretended to be dead. The elephant flipped him over with its tusks to make sure he wasn't moving. Then it trumpeted loudly and walked away.

Jonathan lost a lot of blood and needed 80 stitches in his leg. It was a close call, but he had survived. Staying on the ground and pretending to be dead saved his life.

War Elephants

In ancient times, African elephants were captured and used for warfare. They were trained to handle pain and ignore noise. Armed soldiers rode on their backs during battle. The elephants charged without fear and were difficult to kill. This made them a terrifying force against the enemy!

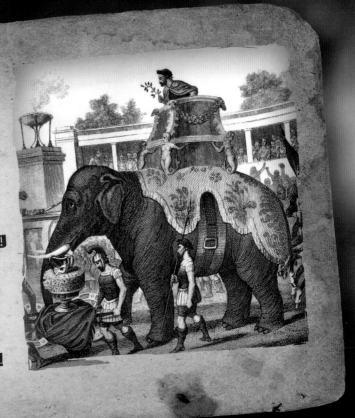

Feet, Trunks, and Tusks

The African elephant is the world's largest land animal. It stands about 11 feet (3.5 meters) tall. That's twice as tall as the average human! At up to 17,600 pounds (8,000 kilograms), an African elephant weighs more than the average school bus. Its size alone makes it dangerous to anyone who comes too close.

Africa

N
W — E
S

African elephant territory =

African elephant

human

Elephants have thick legs and flat, round feet. As they walk, their feet spread out on the ground to support their weight. Padding inside their feet softens each step. This allows elephants to walk almost silently. Their feet can also be deadly. One firmly placed foot will crush a lion trying to take down a young elephant.

A short, muscular neck supports the African elephant's giant head. Its floppy, triangle-shaped ears are larger than those of any other animal. They stretch as wide as 4 feet (1.2 meters). When threatened, elephants spread out their ears to appear bigger. They shake their heads and flap their ears as a warning before they charge.

Elephants breathe and smell through their long, heavy trunks. Their trunks are about 5 feet (1.5 meters) long and weigh more than 300 pounds (136 kilograms). An elephant's trunk has more than 100,000 muscles. With so many muscles, trunks can bend, curl, twist, and reach. They can knock down trees, rip off branches, and lift heavy logs.

Elephants use their trunks the way people use their fingers, hands, and arms. They rub their eyes, scratch an itch, comfort their young, and feed themselves. Elephants can pick up small objects with the two "fingers" at the tip of the trunk. To drink, an elephant sucks water into its trunk and curls the trunk toward its mouth. Then it tilts its head back and pours the water down its throat.

Elephant Herds

African elephants live in groups of about ten related adults and their young. The oldest female is called the matriarch. She leads the herd. Young males eventually leave the herd to live alone or with other males. The females stay together to protect the young.

Trunks can also be powerful weapons. A swing of the trunk can send a lion or a human tumbling. Sometimes an elephant will hold its victim with its trunk and then stab it with a tusk. Elephants can even pick up and throw people with their trunks!

Both male and female elephants have **ivory** tusks. These long, curved teeth grow throughout an elephant's life. Elephants use their tusks to strip bark from trees, unearth roots, and scrape rocks for salt. They also dig their tusks into dry riverbeds in search of water.

Tusks are an elephant's most dangerous weapons. They clash like swords when young males battle for **dominance**. They can also stab and kill lions that threaten their herd or humans who wander into their territory.

Righty or Lefty?

Just as people favor one hand over the other, elephants are either right-tusked or left-tusked. The tusk they use more often wears down faster.

Human Versus Elephant

Huge herds of elephants graze on the plains and in the forests of Africa. To survive, an elephant needs to eat about 300 pounds (136 kilograms) of plants and drink more than 30 gallons (100 liters) of water each day. That means elephants need a lot of room to roam. In recent years, humans have pushed into elephant **habitats**. Roads now cut through their territory, and farmers are taking more land to raise crops.

Elephants have started to push back against humans. They charge into villages in search of food. They stomp crops and knock over huts. In return, farmers shoot at and often kill elephants. Even on lands where elephants are protected, officials kill many of them to keep the herds from growing too big for their shrinking habitats.

Deadly Decline

African elephants are endangered animals. Millions of elephants once lived in Africa, but today only about 300,000 remain.

Like all wild animals, elephants are **unpredictable**. An elephant that is grazing peacefully may suddenly turn violent if it feels threatened. It might trumpet a warning and flap its ears. When the elephant attacks, it charges forward with its ears flat against its head and its trunk between its front legs. The animal knocks its victim to the ground and kicks, stomps, or gores the person.

The best way to be safe in elephant territory is to stay inside a truck or other vehicle. The danger rises for anyone on foot, and there are few ways to escape an angry elephant. Elephants often **bluff** by charging toward a victim and stopping short, but it is risky to stand still. Climbing a large tree is a good way to escape. Throwing a hat or a bag to distract the elephant is another option. If caught, a person should play dead and hope the elephant wanders away.

Elephants can live 65 years or longer, and they have excellent memories. Scientists have discovered that elephants remember when humans have treated them badly. An elephant that saw humans kill one of its family members, break apart its herd, or take over its land may be more violent toward people. Young elephants then learn to be violent toward humans, too.

Some Africans are trying to reduce elephant attacks. They are setting up **eco-tours** to protect elephant habitats while giving visitors the chance to see the animals up close. They take steps to make sure the elephants don't feel threatened. With their help, humans and elephants might one day live in peace.

Attack Facts

- It is estimated that around 500 African elephant attacks occur every year. Around 150 result in death.

- Human-elephant conflicts happen almost daily in Africa. People often evacuate their homes to stay safe.

- In Africa, men tend to stay out later and do more work in the fields than women. Because of this, most victims of elephant attacks are men.

Glossary

bluff—to pretend; African elephants sometimes bluff an attack by charging and then stopping.

dominance—power or control over someone or something; male elephants often fight for dominance of an all-male herd.

eco-tours—guided trips that allow tourists to observe animals and their environment in a way that is safe for both the people and the animals

habitats—the environments in which plants or animals usually live

ivory—hard, white matter that makes up the tusks of elephants and other animals

trumpeting—making a loud sound similar to a trumpet; elephants trumpet with their trunks when they are excited, angry, or lost.

tusks—large, long teeth that stick out of the mouths of some animals

unpredictable—not always behaving in the same way

To Learn More

At the Library

Barnes, Julia. *The Secret Lives of Elephants*. Milwaukee, Wisc.: Gareth Stevens Pub., 2007.

Joubert, Beverly, and Dereck Joubert. *Face to Face with Elephants*. Washington, D.C.: National Geographic, 2008.

Marsh, Laura. *Great Migrations: Elephants*. Washington, D.C.: National Geographic, 2010.

On the Web

Learning more about African elephants is as easy as 1, 2, 3.

1. Go to www.factsurfer.com.

2. Enter "African elephants" into the search box.

3. Click the "Surf" button and you will see a list of related Web sites.

With factsurfer.com, finding more information is just a click away.

Index

The images in this book are reproduced through the courtesy of: Francois van Heerden, front cover, p. 11; Tom & Pat Leeson/KimballStock, pp. 4-5, 18-19; Muriel Hazan/Photolibrary, pp. 6-7; Northwind Picture Archives/Alamy, p. 8; Peter Malsbury/Getty Images, p. 9; Villiers Steyn, p. 13; Christian Heinrich/Alamy, pp. 14-15; Naturfoto-Online/Alamy, pp. 16-17; Hoffmann Photography/Photolibrary, pp. 20-21.